Aung San Suu Kyi

A Selective Bibliography of Dissertations and Theses

Milo Avicenna

Avicenna, Milo

Aung San Suu Kyi: A Selective Bibliography of Dissertations and Theses

p. cm.

1. Aung San Suu Kyi. 2. Pacifism—Religious Aspects--Buddhism. I. Title.

DS 530
959.105

ISBN-10 1977778186

ISBN-13 978-1977778185

Cover Photo - Aung San Suu Kyi

Aung San Suu Kyi

A Selective Bibliography of Dissertations and Theses

Table of Contents

1.)   **Bynum, K. E.**

Multiple discourses: The mobilization of trauma narratives within Burma's Transnational Advocacy Network.

M.A. thesis, Arizona State University. 2011.

Since the 1988 uprising, a transnational advocacy network has formed around the issue of democracy and human rights in Burma. Within this transnational advocacy network, personal narratives of trauma have been promulgated in both international and oppositional news media and human rights reports. My thesis critically analyzes the use of the trauma narrative for advocacy purposes by the transnational advocacy network that has emerged around Burma and reveals the degree to which these narratives adhere to a Western, individualistic meta-narrative focused on political and civil liberties. Examining the "boomerang" pattern and the concept of marketability of movements, I highlight the characteristics of the 1988 uprising and subsequent opposition movement that attracted international interest. Reflecting on the psychological aspects of constructing trauma narratives, I then review the scholarship which links trauma narratives to social and human rights movements. Using a Foucauldian approach to discourse analysis, I subsequently explain my methodology in analyzing the personal narratives I have chosen. Beyond a theoretical discussion of trauma narratives and transnational advocacy networks, I analyze the use of personal narratives of activists involved in the 1988 uprising and the emergence of Aung San Suu Kyi's life story as a compelling narrative for Western audiences. I then explore the structure of human rights reports which situate personal narratives of trauma within the framework of international human rights law. I note the differences in the construction of traumatic narratives of agency and those of victimization. Finally, using Cyclone Nargis as a case study, I uncover the discursive divide between human rights and humanitarian actors and their use of personal narratives to support different discursive constructions of the aid effort in the aftermath of the cyclone. I conclude with an appeal to a more reflexive approach to advocacy work reliant on trauma narratives and highlight feminist methodologies that have been successful in bringing marginalized narratives to the center of human rights discussions. [Author Abstract]

2.)   **Cukingnan, N. C.**

The evolution of the media in the Aung San Suu Kyi saga from 1988-2013.

M.A.L.S. thesis, Georgetown University. 2013.

This thesis aims to examine the evolution of the media in the Aung San Suu Kyi saga to show the changes that have taken place, from the dominance of print media at the beginning of her struggle for democracy in 1988 to the growing role of digital media by 2013. Technological advancements have allowed digital media to be fast, far-reaching, and pervasive. The media has thus been an important tool in impacting change in Burma, from military rule to some civilian rule. The term Burma will be used in the thesis until 1989, when the military junta changed the country's name to Myanmar. The scope covers a period of twenty-four years and includes the media chronicling her return home in 1989 to care for her ailing mother, winning the 1990 elections and the 1991 Nobel Peace Prize, and being elected to parliament in 2012 as her country's most notable democratic leader. The organization of this thesis is in five parts. Chapter I, "Introduction: Background Information to 1988 on the Media, Burma (Myanmar), and Aung San Suu Kyi," sets the stage by providing important relevant information for the rest of this thesis. Chapter II, "The Role of Print and Broadcast Media in the Aung San Suu Kyi Saga, 1989-1990," tracks the beginning of her relationship with the media and shows how they reinforce each other. The media provided her a platform to voice her country's struggles and she afforded the media compelling stories on human rights abuses. Chapter III, "The Continued Domination of Print and Broadcast Media in the Aung San Suu Kyi Saga, 1991-1999," continues to explore this relationship by focusing on socio-economic and political problems in Myanmar as well as on the media's role. Chapter IV, "Aung San Suu Kyi and the Media, 2000-2011," examines some long-awaited changes in Myanmar along with the growth of digital media, which captured and immediately relayed these historic events. Chapter V, "Conclusion: The Media's Role in the Aung San Suu Kyi Saga, 2012-2013, and Future Prospects," traces the latest developments in media coverage of Myanmar and Aung San Suu Kyi and discusses some future prospects regarding her and the media. [Author Abstract]

3.)   **Davies, J. A.**

An experiential inquiry into the intersubjective principles of Relational Dharma as exemplified in Aung San Suu Kyi's spiritual revolution.
Ph.D. dissertation, Saybrook University. 2010.

Research into intersubjectivity as a formative determiner in factors of human growth through reciprocal co-influence is recognized across disciplines ranging from physical theories to psychological models. This qualitative study elaborates an experiential model of intersubjectivity: Relational Dharma. The research question was, "What are the indicators (principles, perspectives and/or practices) that may inform a transdisciplinary path for an understanding of higher human relatedness?" This study includes: (a) an investigation into intersubjectivity from selective interdisciplinary perspectives and theories, and (b) utilizing heuristic methodology as outlined by Moustakas (heuristic research), a content analysis was conducted of archival interviews. The data used to answer the research question were derived from audio taped interviews with primary participant Nobel Peace Prize laureate and leader of Burma's non-violent struggle for democratic freedom, Aung San Suu Kyi, and her two key colleagues U Tin Oo and U Kyi Maung. The interviews were conducted between October 1995 and June 1996 inside of her home during a brief period of freedom following her first six years of incarceration. Dharma is a Sanskrit Buddhist word that refers to the specific elements and natural processes that govern experience. Relational Dharma re-envisions the teaching of dependent origination (paticca samuppada) as an intersubjective architecture that can be understood through the development of insight within shared awareness in human relationship. An intersubjective theme of higher human relatedness (HHR), as developed by the author, refers to forms of expression within human interaction that arise through this progression of insight. Twenty-five intersubjective themes of HHR emerged from the data: genuine spiritual change; freedom; non-violence; loving-kindness and compassion; karma; interdependence; impermanence; unity; wholeness; spiritual strength; power; wisdom; an open questioning mind; courage and determination; truth, truthfulness and honesty; awareness; virtue; patience; fearlessness; generosity; responsibility; humanizing the other; good friendship; humor and joy; and forgiveness. Through the exploration of Relational Dharma as a path to release from conditions that lead to suffering through insight into interrelatedness and illumination of the wisdom that exemplifies the realization of interrelatedness, this research reveals a framework for higher human relatedness imbued with a uniquely universal, spiritual wisdom. [Author Abstract]

4.)   **DeYoung, C. P.**

Mystic-activists: Faith-inspired leaders working for social justice and reconciliation.
Ed.D. dissertation, University of St. Thomas (Minnesota). 2004.

This study examined social justice leaders from the twentieth century who discovered their vision and reason for activism through their faith. The faith-inspired activists included in this study were not typically mystics or contemplatives in the purest sense. The call to activism consumed them. Yet their activism compelled them to passionately reach inward for sustenance, wisdom, perseverance, and a sense of belonging. Their activism needed mysticism. Three social justice activists were the primary focus: Dietrich Bonhoeffer, Malcolm X, and Aung San Suu Kyi. These three individuals offered a wide range in time periods, cultural settings, genders, and faith traditions. While these three were the central figures in this study, the viewpoints and life experiences of others from the twentieth century were incorporated, including Martin Luther King Jr., Rigoberta Menchú, Nelson Mandela, Winona LaDuke, Oscar Romero, Fannie Lou Hamer, Elie Wiesel, Mohandas Gandhi, Dorothy Day, Desmond Tutu, Thich Nhat Hanh, Abraham Heschel, Allan Boesak, and the Dalai Lama. The methods used were not solely biographical or historical research. With a bias for social change, what Sara Lawrence-Lightfoot called "social science portraiture" best described the methodology. A number of shared themes— or ways of being—became apparent from this study of the lives of faith-inspired social justice activists. Four themes appeared, to varying degrees, in each of the lives of the three principle leaders: (1) they were motivated by their religious faith; (2) they had a worldview that emerged from the margins of society; (3) their identity was rooted in a belief that we share a common humanity; and (4) they embraced an ethics of revolution that demanded structural change. The argument is made that these four ways of being are also critical for empowering leaders in the twenty-first century who work for reconciliation with justice in a multicultural, multi-faith, multi-perspective world. [Author Abstract]

5.)   **Giannessi, B.**

Theoretical and Textual Approaches to Contemporary Humanitarian Narrative: The cases of Roberto Saviano's Gomorra, Aung San Suu Kyi's Letters from Burma, Jerry Piasecki's Marie in the Shadow of the Lion and Nadine Gordimer's The Ultimate Safari.

Ph.D. dissertation, Pisa University (Italy). 2012.

The purpose of this thesis is to describe how some forms of fictional and non-fictional texts can be configured as and within the framework of humanitarian practices. In exploring the definitions and features of humanitarianism and humanitarian literature, the thesis attempts to answer the question of what purpose these texts try to serve. In examining the works *Marie in the Shadow of the Lion* (2000) by Jerry Piasecki, *The Ultimate Safari* (1989) by Nadine Gordimer, *Gomorra* (2006) by Roberto Saviano and *Letters from Burma* (1996) by Aung San Suu Kyi, we will argue that the scope of these books can be located by analogy to social and political humanitarian practices. Beyond their differences in genre, style and subject matter, these texts share a common feature: they are performative, namely they strive to do things with words. The humanitarian texts discussed in this thesis can be shown to act in the world in order to implement the values proclaimed in the Universal Declaration of Human Rights. [Author Abstract]

6.)   **Gorsevski, E. W.**

The geopolitics of peaceful persuasion: Toward a theory of nonviolent rhetoric.
Ph.D. dissertation, The Pennsylvania State University. 1999.

This dissertation lays a conceptual and philosophical foundation for developing a theory of nonviolent rhetoric. Much analysis and knowledge exist concerning hate rhetoric and war rhetoric, but there are few studies of nonviolent rhetoric and rhetorics of peace-makers. There is a need for recognizing the social, cultural, and political value of nonviolence in fostering justice in contemporary democracies. Chapter 2 takes a public address approach to rhetorical criticism in light of a theory of nonviolence. It discusses the pragmatic nonviolent approach to rhetoric and public address of the President of Macedonia, Kiro Gligorov, at Macedonia's new nationhood in 1993 and in light of Kosovo, 1999. Pragmatic nonviolent rhetoric exhibits a long-term view to peace-making. Chapter 3 examines the visual rhetoric of Aung San Suu Kyi, Nobel Peace Prize winner and democratic opposition party leader in Myanmar (Burma). Her oratorical skills are impressive, and she has a prodigious public speaking career by any standard of success in public address. However, it is her essentialized persona that is most interesting. Her nonviolent uses of her physical body, combined with her photogenic beauty, vital in this electronic age, create unique rhetorical success and risks for her nonviolent campaign promoting democracy and an end to Burma's military dictatorship. Chapter 4 examines diffuse rhetoric of a nonviolent social movement. The concept of a rhetorical climate is posited. Climates of feeling/experience can be as persuasive as written texts and other forms of symbolic rhetoric. Rhetoric surrounding nonviolent action in Montana, 1993, is analyzed. An entire town rose to the occasion and peacefully prevailed over neo-nazi hate crimes and terrorism. In short, this dissertation surveys how nonviolent theory supports the notion that humans can argue fairly and arrive at mutual understanding through a risky proms of tolerance and self-conversion. Nonviolent activists' unique choices and creativity in persuading shows the rhetorical power of using satyagraha (soul-force) to create a healthy environment to foster social change and equality. [Author Abstract]

7.)   **Grønkjær, L.**

Myanmar's democratic transition: An examination of internal and external factors leading Myanmar's military regime to commence on a transition toward democracy.
M.S. thesis, Roskilde University (Denmark). 2015.

Since the inauguration of President Thein Sein in March 2011, Myanmar has adopted remarkable democratic reforms in a transition from military to democratic rule. Informed by the literature on democratic transitions, this thesis examines which factors motivated Myanmars military regime to commence on a transition towards democracy. This examination of Myanmars democratic transition is structured around an identified division between competing arguments within the literature on democratic transitions. One group of scholars emphasise the importance of internal factors as decisive when authoritarian regimes transition towards democracy, while another group of scholars emphasise external factors. Through a deductive research strategy, concepts emphasising internal and external factors will be applied to the case of Myanmars democratic transition, in order to comprehensively assess which of these two competing arguments best explain Myanmars democratic transition. I found that internal factors are best applied to the case of Myanmars regime-controlled transition. A political momentum for regime softliners to instigate democratic reforms was identified, as perceived threats had decreased, key interests were safeguarded and an elite pact was established between President Thein Sein and Aung San Suu Kyi. I found that external factors were unable to explain Myanmars democratic transition, as there was not found a link between democratisation and socioeconomic development, and CSOs had a minimal impact on instigating democratic reforms. Moreover, I found that while economic sanctions were unable to create regime change through economic punishment, they indirectly impacted the democratic transition through increased dependence on China. [Author Abstract]

8.)   **Ho, T. C.**

Through a Burmese looking-glass:
Transgression, displacement, and transnational
women's identities.
Ph.D. dissertation, University of California, Los
Angeles. 2005.

Using Burma as a unifying example, this
dissertation traces how gendered racial identities
are articulated against each other. The Burmese
women examined here write against their
material and discursive "prisons" by using
"flexible tactics of displacement" to counter
competing systems of authority; Western
ideologies and Burmese cultural signifiers
become tools used to disrupt intersecting
repressive hegemonies. Part I highlights the
"damage" done to Burmese female subjectivities
by Westernization and "modernity" by comparing
George Orwell's *Burmese Days* to Ma Ma Lay's
Not Out of Hate; Part II focuses on Aung San
Suu Kyi and Wendy Law-Yone's *Irrawaddy Tango*
to illustrate how Burmese women tactically and

flexibly invoke the global/West to serve local and "minor" agendas. Maneuvering between Orientalism and globalization and demonstrating discursive dexterity in transnational circuits of power, Burmese women translate their discursive imprisonment into states of productive constraint. Chapter 1 demonstrates how *Burmese Days* illustrates the displacement of Burmese women and prefigures the rise of venal masculinity in contemporary Myanmar. The novel's portrait of Late British imperial Burma lays the foundation for Burmese women's invisibility and hypervisibility. Chapter 2 tracks how *Not Out of Hate* articulates writing and Buddhism as feminized spaces of resistance against a deleterious "modern" patriarchal paradigm that forces Burmese women and "tradition" into positions of subordination. Chapter 3 compares representations of Aung San Suu Kyi with how she writes herself. The Burmese democratic leader transforms androcentric paradigms to serve her agenda of change and reconciliation. Utilizing and deconstructing familiar notions of identity, nation, and gender, Aung San Suu Kyi tactically combines global and local discourses to articulate her "flexible" politics of resistance. Chapter 4 analyzes Wendy Law-Yone's portrayal of Third World women as survivors defying Western and Asian regimes of authority. *Irrawaddy Tango* explores how authority, cruelty, and oppression on both sides of the Pacific reflect each other. Law-Yone reframes "subaltern" agency and explicates the dilemma of crafting an ethnic minority subject position for Burmese in the West. In conclusion, I recap how Burmese women use diverse cultural grammars toward liberatory ends and outline how these narratives of Burma critique complacency, hegemony, and power. [Author Abstract]

9.) **Hoffmann, M. R.**

Towards a global rhetoric: Theory, practice, pedagogy.

Ph.D. dissertation, University of Maryland, College Park. 2014.

This dissertation works towards building a theory of "global rhetoric" as well as practical strategies for both using and teaching global rhetorical principles. Global rhetoric, as I suggest, describes argumentation that maintains persuasive potential for audiences beyond the rhetor's immediate location and time. I build this theory of global rhetoric by offering three "case studies" of exemplary global rhetorical texts: Leo Tolstoy's *The Kingdom of God Is Within You* (1893), Randolph Bourne's *The State* (1919), and Aung San Suu Kyi's *In Quest of Democracy* (1991). In each of these case studies, I pay particular attention to the rhetorical tactics that drive the arguments of the essays as well as to the sets of appeals that would maintain persuasive potential as they reached broad, vast, and dispersed audiences. I bring this analysis to bear on everyday needs. I examine how professional business communicators can use global rhetorical strategies in their work in order to communicate and persuade more effectively across borders and cultures. To this end, I offer a case study of how a multimodal business presentation was revised to better address global audiences. Finally, I suggest how we can better teach both first- and second-language writing students to be global rhetors. I outline a professional writing course—Professional Global Rhetoric—and I offer both a pedagogical rationale and ready-to-use assignment sheets. These assignment sheets are designed to enable writing instructors and Writing Program Administrators to launch a course that builds upon the principles of global rhetoric. The argument put forth in this dissertation builds from the longstanding rhetorical notion that argumentation is a situated, circumstantial practice that is shaped by the audience. What a global rhetoric suggests, I argue, is that rhetors can look beyond their immediate rhetorical situations and deliberately construct arguments to maintain persuasive potential for audiences across geographic borders and through time. [Author Abstract]

10.)   **Johansen, T.**

ASEAN's incorporation of Burma - a hidden agenda?: A study of the motives behind the inclusion of Burma in ASEAN (Translated from Norwegian)

M.S. thesis, University of Oslo (Norway). 1999.

In this exercise, I have analyzed the motives behind the process that led to the inclusion of Burma in ASEAN in 1997. The inclusion was highly controversial and was strongly criticized by the United States and the EU. There was also strong resistance to finding among NGOs in both Asia and Europe. Likewise, the Burmese opposition both inside and outside Burma, with Aung San Suu Kyi in the head, strongly opposed an incorporation at that time. In spite of this, a single ASEAN chose to occupy Burma in the community. The inclusion of Burma was justified by ASEAN with the need to continue their "constructive commitment" towards Burma. Since 1991, ASEAN has pursued a policy aimed at developing increased economic and political contact with the military regime in Burma, publicly motivated by the fact that in the long term this may lead Burma into a more democratic political system. The problem of the task was therefore to analyze the extent to which it was a "constructive engagement policy" which was the real cause of ASEAN's decision to incorporate Burma into membership. My starting point was to see if the "constructive engagement policy" was the actual motive or whether it was temporary. After the analysis, I can conclude that reasons other than the desire to pursue a constructive commitment towards Burma, explained more that a single ASEAN chose to bring Burma at that time. There were other motives behind. China's close relationship with Burma and its strong position against the ASEAN countries could explain a large part of the motive for an incorporation. In addition, I found support for the purely economic interests of the ASEAN countries in Burma. At the same time it was also clear that ASEAN would not be dictated by the West as a result of pressure on a postponement.

Asian values versus Western values, with the desire to develop a regional identity in ASEAN among the new countries, were therefore central to the final phase of the incorporation process. The use of an eclectic approach to the study of ASEAN was very fruitful. The decision on incorporation had several reasons. Nyrealism has an overly unilateral perception of the world system as a struggle for survival and fears of states to enter into cooperation with other states. A weakness of the theory was that it did not capture the positive perception of the possibilities for cooperation. This was complemented by the use of contributions within neoliberal institutionalism, emphasizing the effect of existing norms and rules on promoting cooperation. The two rationalist perspectives were supplemented with theories that focus on the individual level. An analysis of the world from just a power balance of thought or from institutional powers would omit an understanding of identity and belonging, represented by reflective theories. The theory turned out to be able to explain a large part of the motives in the final phase of the incorporation process. By using international political theories that captured various causes and levels, this eclectic approach contributed to a comprehensive picture of the incorporation process. [Author Abstract]

11.)   **Lian, E. S.**

Conscience formation and faithful citizenship in Burma after the model of Aung San Suu Kyi.
M.A. thesis, Saint Louis University. 2017.

I argue in this thesis how Aung San Suu Kyi though a Buddhist can play an important role or proves a perfect model in conscience formation of the citizens of Burma that is in line with the Catholic Church's moral teaching. I am presenting her as a model in conscience formation by first providing the context of Burma where the consciences of citizens need to be ignited in order to become good and responsible citizens. Burma went through the military dictatorship rule for nearly 50 years. As a result, lives of citizens of Burma became not only poor economically but also decreased morally, which resulted in poor participation in politics. Amidst this situation, consciences seem dormant and need revival. For this, I use Catholic Moral Theologian Richard M. Gula whose arguments for conscience formation prove suitable to apply to

Burmese context. Gula emphasizes social nature and context in his argument for conscience formation. In addition, his approach is holistic meaning he incorporates the intellect, the will, the mind, and the physical and the social dimensions of conscience formation in his argument. He is also faithful to the Catholic Church's teaching, which proves his theology sound and trustworthy to apply. I then incorporate Gula's main ideas into Suu Kyi's life mainly arguing that she is the perfect model for the citizens of Burma in conscience formation to become good and responsible citizens. She most of all can prove this by/through her good education, good character, broad vision, and love for her country. I then argue that the Catholic Church in Burma can use Suu Kyi as a model to imitate in conscience formation. What the Church can practically do in this regard is advocate holistic education as a step for conscience formation with the intention that Burmese citizens can become good and responsible citizens grounded in good education and moral character. This thesis serves as the basic foundation for Burmese citizens to think about in their conscience formation of becoming good and responsible citizens. [Author Abstract]

12.)   **Mitchell, K. L.**

The extraordinary woman: Engendering Max Weber's theory of charisma.
Ph.D. dissertation, University of Missouri, Kansas City. 2006.

Max Weber presents a typology of ideal types of power---charismatic, traditional, and legal-rational. Men historically have been the basis for Weber's and other scholar's theories. Today, there are enough women in political positions to construct a typology on the effects of gender on power and authority. My dissertation suggests that the type of system through which women come to power determines the role of gender on access to power but that the exercise of legitimate authority remains upon cultural norms. My typology offers an explanation for the anomalies that arise for women seeking political power. The legal-rational system has been well studied. It is a non-gendered institution located in culturally determined eligibility pools. Once women fill the qualifications for participation in the eligibility pool, there is the possibility for political access. Women in traditional political systems come to power only in the absence of a male heir but do not exercise authority in their own right. The cultural expectation for women is this system is to marry and produce male heirs. The husband is the authority. Charisma demands that the leader exhibit extraordinary powers. There are, however, traditional leaders who have exercised political authority and there are charismatic women leaders. The eligibility pool for charismatic women is the traditional system. The charismatic relationship allows the woman in the traditional system to exercise authority. For women, there are two ideal sources of power--- legal-rational and traditional. Legitimate authority, however, rests upon the support of law in the legal-rational system for both men and women. Legitimate authority in the traditional system is supported by the charismatic relationship between a leader and her followers. I focus on three modern-political women---Aung San Suu Kyi of Burma, Chandrika

Kumaratunga of Sri Lanka, and Benazir Bhutto of Pakistan---whose circumstances present enough similarities to allow for the discovery of equivalencies of charisma through comparative political analysis. [Author Abstract]

13.)   **Murphree, D. P.**

Imagining the Buddhist Ecumene in Myanmar: How Buddhist paradigms dictate belonging in contemporary Myanmar

M.S. thesis, University of Washington. 2017.

This paper argues that the model of an Ecumene will aid external interpretation of the Myanmar political process, including the beliefs of its leaders and constituents, the Bamar. Myanmar as Ecumene better articulates Bama constructions of society, including governance, in that it resituates the political process as a Buddhist enterprise, shifting Buddhist nationalism to an imagined Nation of Buddhists. It also provides the rationale for othering of religious minorities, such as the Muslim Rohingya or the Christian Chin. Utilizing ethnographic, historical, and textual source material, I show how the Bamar of Myanmar understand their relationship with the State, with one another, and with minority groups primarily through Buddhist modes of kingship and belonging. The right to rule is negotiated through the concept of moral authority. This dhamma sphere exists as a space to contest power legitimation, but requires the use of Buddhist textual and historical concepts provided in the dhammaraja or Cakkavattin model of Buddhist kingship, The Ten Virtues, the Jatakas, and the historical figures of Asoka and Anawrahta. In order to do this, this paper develops a rubric for interpreting what a dhammaraja does. This has not been done before and will allow the reader the ability to evaluate whether or not any given government in Myanmar is operating according to a dhammaraja tradition. Based on the rubric provided and source materials, this paper concludes that Daw Aung San Suu Kyi, presumed leader of Myanmar, imagines herself a Buddhist dhammaraja and the leader of a Buddhist Ecumene. The Bamar are concerned about the decline of dhamma and the retraction of a Buddhist land, and this concern provides a basis of support and concern for the current regime. [Author Abstract]

14.) **Parameshwar, S.**

Birthing new worlds through exceptional responses to challenging circumstances.
Ph.D. dissertation, Case Western Reserve University. 2001.

The author seeks to uncover the exceptional responses through which eleven internationally renowned leaders of human rights brought forth new worlds into existence by their discontinuous engagement with the challenging circumstances that they encountered. The dissertation undertakes an in-depth examination of the autobiographies and biographies of Mother Teresa, Mahatma Gandhi, Hellen Keller, Kwame Nkrumah, Karl Marx, Harriet Tubman, Aung San Suu Kyi, Viktor Frankl, Rigoberta Menchu, Nawal El Saadawi, and Paulo Freire. The study focuses its theoretical lens on these individuals' discontinuous engagement with their challenging circumstances as manifested in their exceptional responses, and the consequences of responding exceptionally for these individuals and for the world touched by their exceptional responses. The dissertation also contains a review of the pertinent scholarly literature highlighting the perspectives of behavioral scientists on the exceptional dimensions of human behavior. The method is alternatively deductive and inductive; it is deductive inasmuch as the notion of exceptional responses embedded in the author's model guided her inquiry, but it is inductive inasmuch as specific hypotheses about exceptional responses were deferred until data collection was underway. The author adapted devices from grounded theory and from transcendental phenomenology; she used methodological devices from the former in the selection of her sample and in her analysis, and used devices from the latter in her analysis. The exceptional responses made by the individuals to the challenging circumstances they faced constitute the unit of analysis. The series of exceptional responses made by these individuals to the challenging circumstances they encountered over their lifetime-on-display-in-their-autobiography, captures the progressive unfolding of the phenomena of interest. The author integrates the uniformities underlying the particularistic aspects of exceptional responses yielded by this vertical within-autobiography analysis, as well as, the uniformities underlying the universal aspects of exceptional responses, through a horizontal across-autobiographies analysis, into a theory-in-process of Birthing New Worlds Through Exceptional Responses to Challenging Circumstances. [Author Abstract]

15.)   **Patel, J. H.**

A Burkean analysis of Aung San Suu Kyi's leadership role in the political development of Burma.

M.A. thesis, The University of Texas, Pan American. 2000.

The focus of this thesis is the historical and analytical role, influence and effect of Aung San, U Nu, and Ne Win in the struggle of independent post-war Burma between the philosophy of Buddhism and the aims of a Socialist welfare-state and its effect on Aung San Suu Kyi's struggle for democracy in present day Burma. There has not been any rhetorical analysis of Aung San Suu Kyi as of yet. Chapter 1 covers the political history of Burma in detail; it will cover the monarchy period, the British colonization, and the struggle for independence. Chapter 2 will concentrate on the cultural developments of India and Burma under colonial rule and Chapter 3 covers the historic role of Buddhism, as a religion, social structure, and resistance to secularism. Chapter 4 consists of the analysis of Aung San's political ideologies and the examination of the influences he had during the struggle for independence, the present effects, and the foundations for the next era. Chapter 5 analyzes U Nu and Ne Win's role, religious influence and outcome of their leadership role in the political development of the nation. Chapter 6 will cover of Aung San Suu Kyi's political ideologies and her ability to lead the nation to their second independence. [Author Abstract]

16.)   **Perry, K. J.**

The gentle general: An examination of leadership strategies and tactics in nonviolent direct action campaigns.

M.A. thesis, Western Illinois University. 2013.

The following thesis aims to broaden the research on nonviolent direct action (NVDA) by examining the role of leadership in successful nonviolent campaigns. The paper will begin with an overview of the method of NVDA and discuss in detail the common strategies and tactics used in nonviolent campaigns. The background on NVDA will then be applied to the case studies of Mahatma Gandhi, Dr. Martin Luther King, Jr., Nelson Mandela and Aung San Suu Kyi. These case studies will outline the individual journeys of each leader and discuss which strategies and tactics were chosen and why as well as how each leader viewed their respective opponent and why they believed nonviolent methods would be successful. This section will wrap up with a brief discussion on the contributing legacy to NVDA left by Gandhi, King, and Mandela. In the discussion section, the paper will bring together the major highlights of NVDA and the strategies that have proven the most successful. It will then present the author's conclusion that the role of leadership is the most vital element to a successful nonviolent direct action campaign. This conclusion will be applied to the campaign in Burma led by Aung San Suu Kyi and suggest ways in which the application of varying strategies can strengthen her leadership role and facilitate a nonviolent future for the country. [Author Abstract]

17.)   **Saifey, T.**

A framework for leadership: Analyzing the struggles of Aung San Suu Kyi.
M.P.S. thesis, The George Washington University. 2011.

There are unique forces at play that drive and sustain women in leadership roles in the East: In the case of Aung San Suu Kyi these have been the qualities of fearlessness, forgiveness, an ability to live in the paradox between her sense of traditional duty and social unconventionalities and her constant connection with both her own region's non-violent traditions and a wider perspective of political possibilities. [Author Abstract]

18.)   **Tan, C. N.**

*Legitimacy, coercion and economic development:
A study of the military regime in Burma.*
M.A. thesis, The University of Regina (Canada).
2004.

In Burma, the military or the *Tatmadaw* has staged three coups since its independence. As of 1988, the country has been ruled directly by a military junta. Burmese prodemocracy leader Aung San Suu Kyi and her National League for Democracy (NLD) party won a landslide victory in the 1990 general elections, but was denied power by the military regime. After years of on-and-off political arrest, harassment and constant surveillance, Aung San Suu Kyi has remained committed in her peaceful campaign for democratic transition to civilian rule in the country. In May 2003, she was placed under house arrest for the third time. The dominance of the military regime in Burma raises questions on the tenacity of authoritarianism and the use of coercion to remain in power. What explains the durability of the military regime in Burma? This thesis attempts an answer by applying a structure-agent approach at both the local and international levels to explain the resilience of the various Burmese military regimes in power since 1962. Based on an explanatory framework that posits legitimacy, coercion, and economic development as three interrelated variables, a list of hypotheses was created to assess and explain the possible factors contributing to the resilience of the military regime in Burma. While most theories have suggested that coercion and brute force is the key reason to explain the durability of the military regime in Burma, this thesis argues that both coercive and non-coercive means have been employed by the various regimes to legitimize and prolong their rule. Besides coercion, the military leadership has employed legitimacy-bases such as nationalism. Buddhism and the idea of the military as "guardian" and "state-builder" to sustain its "right to rule." As the legitimation of power process is interactive and dynamic, the stalling efforts in liberalizing the formerly autarkic economy and reliance on state coercion to obtain compliance have undermined the ruling regime's "performance legitimacy." This study posits that it is highly unlikely Burma will transit to 'objective civilian control' in the near future. The lack of interactive channels between the rulers and ruled to negotiate a power-sharing arrangement and economic mismanagement could precipitate a "legitimacy crisis" for the ruling military regime.   [Author Abstract]

19.) **Yip, N.**

Moving beyond Rangoon: The construction of disabled bodies in twentieth-century colonial, postcolonial, and Asian American literature.
Ph.D. dissertation, The George Washington University. 2007.

This study encompasses the fields of Disability Studies, Asian American Studies and Postcolonial Studies. I examine the intersections between Asian American and Postcolonial literature through Disabilities Studies, which considers issues of able-bodiedness and normalcy, against which certain identities and characteristics are considered deviant, disabled and disruptive. I examine the ways in which compulsory heterosexuality has been working in and around these three fields of study by considering how heteronormativity fails because queerness is also working in and around these three fields of discourse. I move Disability Studies further into

Globalization Studies with an inclusive analysis of Asian American and Postcolonial theory and literature. To situate Disability Studies as a theoretical link between Asian American and Postcolonial literature, I move beyond the established, Orientalizing narratives of Burma, and examine the colonial body, the colonized body and the postcolonial body to position disability as a unifying trope that at the same time shows different material and historical conditions. I examine George Orwell's *Burmese Days*, Jade Snow Wong's *Fifth Chinese Daughter* and Helie Lee's *Still Life with Rice* to analyze compulsory systems of heterosexuality and able-bodiedness, theories from Adrienne Rich and Robert McRuer, respectively, to set up Disability Studies as a linking field. I discuss Wendy Law-Yone's *The Coffin Tree* to connect Postcolonial and Asian American literature. I analyze Ma Ma Lay's *Not Out of Hate*, Aung San Suu Kyi in *Freedom From Fear* and *Letters from Burma*, and

Pascal Khoo Thwe in *From the Land of Green Ghosts: A Burmese Odyssey*, to describe the various kinds of disabled bodies being produced from colonial Burma to the present-day authoritarian, Burmese military government. [Author Abstract]

Locating Dissertations and Theses

A. Purchase

Many of the dissertations and theses listed in this bibliography are available for purchase through UMI Dissertation Express:

http://disexpress.umi.com/dxweb

By Fax:

800-864-0019

By Mail:

789 E. Eisenhower Parkway, P.O. Box 1346, Ann Arbor, Michigan 48106-1346

800-521-3042

B. Interlibrary Loan

Dissertations and theses may also be requested through Interlibrary Loan via your local public, college or university library.